Black Apple Phoetry

Joep Rous

DEDICATION

For all women in my life.

CONTENTS

Acknowledgments   i

Preface   ii

Brand new   1

Top view   2

After the rain   3

Drops   4

Heavy rain   5

Patterns   6

Sparkles   7

Icy hat   8

Coastal line   9

Below zero   10

Icy crystals   11

Ice and snow   12

Covered in snow   13

Melting snow   14

Slush   15

Dust   16

Dirt   17

Pollen   18

Walnut   19

Reflection   20

Frosty reflection   21

Morning dew   22

Dazzling dew   23

Black dew   24

Frozen dew   25

Moonlight   26

Garden lights   27

Pitch black	28
Sunset	29
Shadow	30
Wasp	31
Spider	32
Caterpillar	33
Snail	34
Dead bodies	35
Gerbera daisy	36
Silver strings	37
Acrobats	38
Pigeon shit	39
Leaf	40
Real thing	41
42	42

ACKNOWLEDGEMENTS

I would like to thank my wife Jeanne for pushing me to take up photography again and for letting me use her black glass apple in our garden ☺. I also would like to thank Hanneke and all members of "Fotocollectief Contrast" for their comments and encouragements to complete this project.

PREFACE

In this book photography and poetry are like twins. Each twin of photo and poem was born on the same day, although most of the time the photo was first. The photo served as inspiration, created the context and determined the theme of the poem. Now, after their creation, they really strengthen each other. Without the poems the book would be "just" a photo book. Without the photos most poems would lack context and would be hard to interpret. This is the reason why I called it "Phoetry", the book is a blend of Photography and Poetry.

Except for the "Real thing" all photographs show the same object:: a small black glass apple in my garden. This book illustrates how different the photos of such a simple yet elegant object can become.

> An apple can have many faces.
> Each of them a big surprise.
> The rain, the wind, the snow it faces.
> Create an apple in disguise.

I hope the reader will enjoy this book as much as I enjoyed creating the photographs and the poems.

October 1st 2015,
Joep Rous

1 BRAND NEW

No spots no wrinkles.
No creases no crinkles.
No wear no tear.
Purity is fair yet rare.

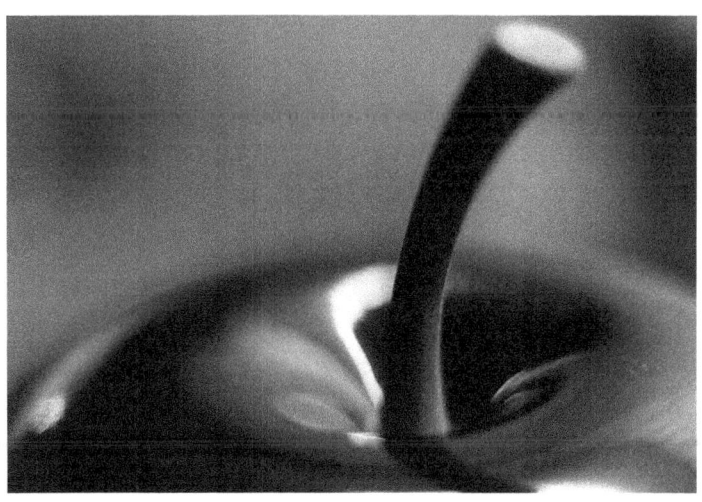

2 TOP VIEW

When viewed from above the apple looks strange.
Nothing about that we're able to change.
She is not blonde but black, not hairy but bald.
Yet if you call her ugly I would be appalled!

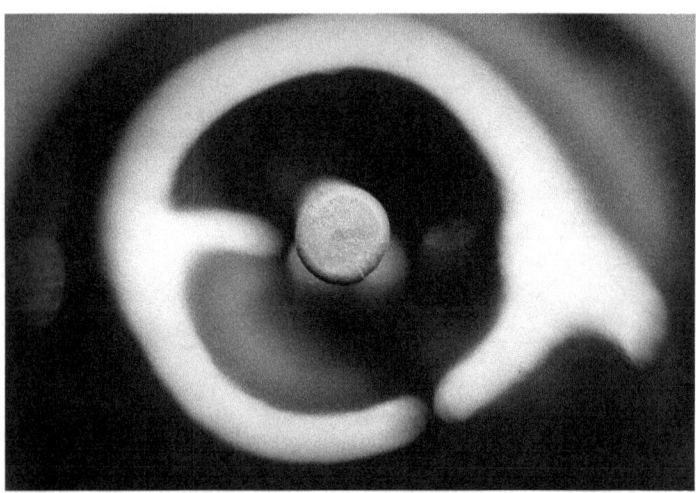

3 AFTER THE RAIN

Rain filled up the dimple.
A tiny pond.
An escaping wand.
Beautiful and simple.

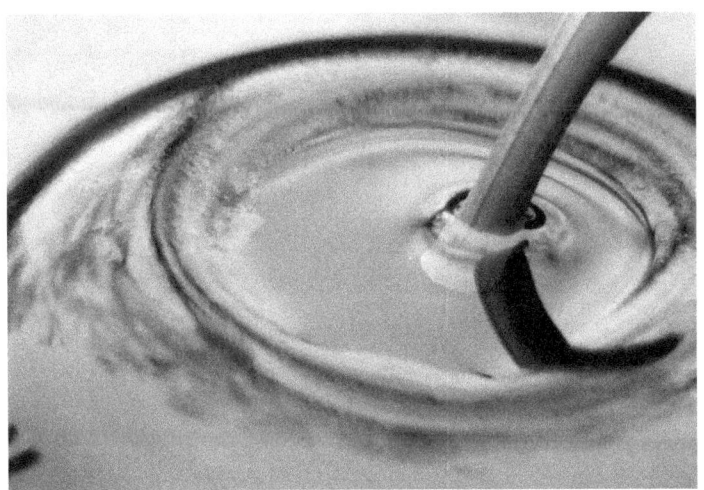

4 DROPS

Rain was here.
Fat drops are sticking to the glass.
Not sliding down.
Defying gravity with heavy mass.

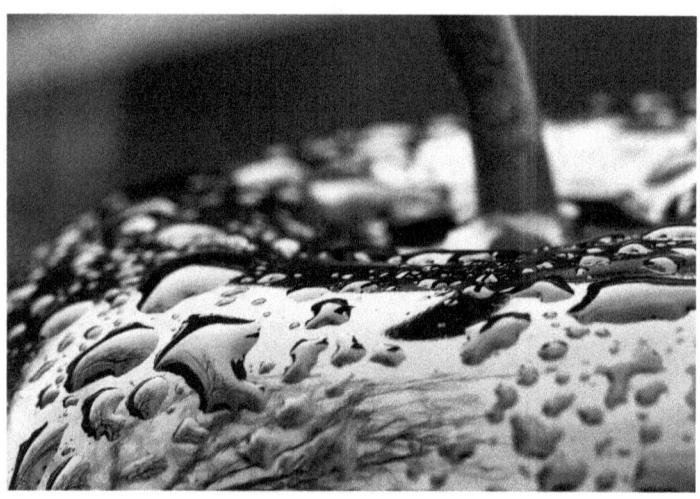

5 HEAVY RAIN

The storm is fierce, the rain intense.
How long will darkness last?
When will the sun unfold its light
for us to have a blast?

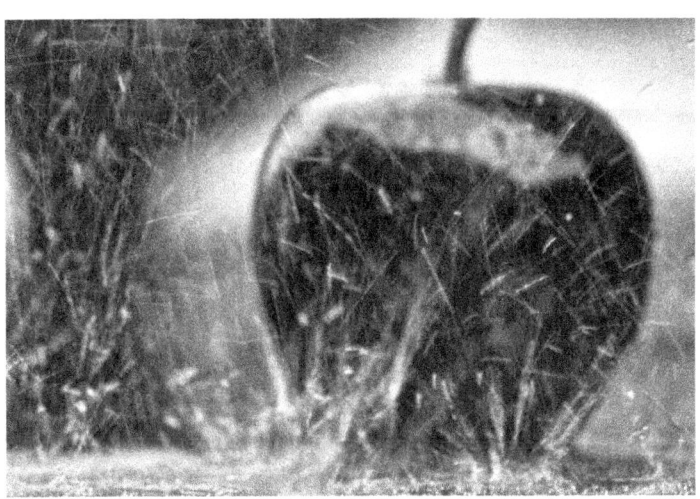

6 PATTERNS

Nature pulls one of its magic tricks
with a droplet/reflection mix.
Next, she adds some shadow and light
to make a perfect black & white.

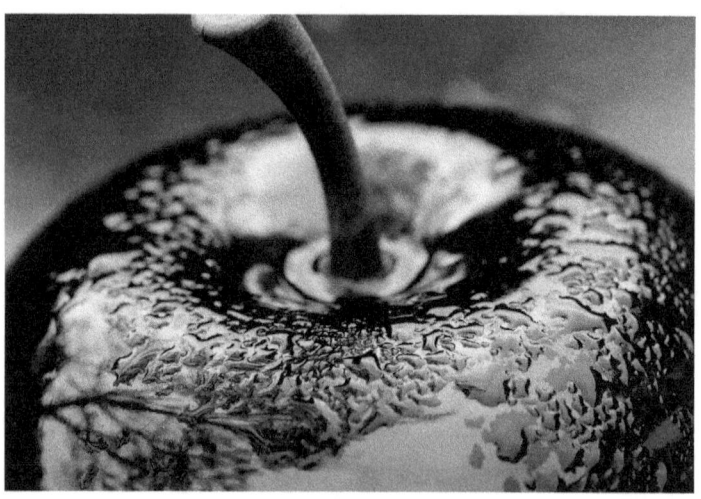

7 SPARKLES

Crystals scattering the light of the sun.
A rainbow of colors increasing the fun.
The apple enfolded in a magic carpet.
So splendid, so gorgeous, so hard to forget.

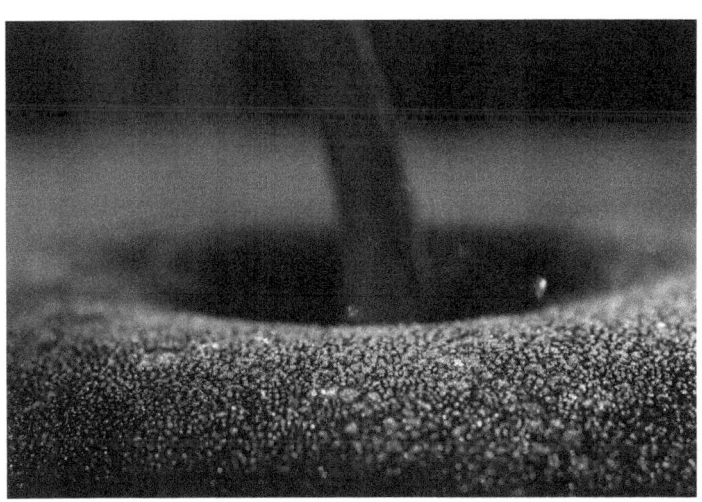

8 ICY HAT

An icy hat after a winter night.
The sun is rising, the nature quiet.
Rays are touching the hat so white.
Trying to lift it with tender light.

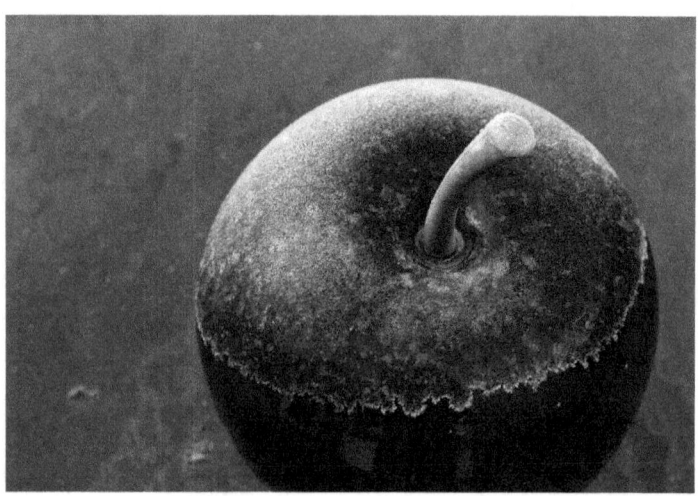

9 COASTAL LINE

Nature creates fractal structures.
Resembling a coastal line.
The North Pole sticks out as a land mark.
I own this new land it is mine!

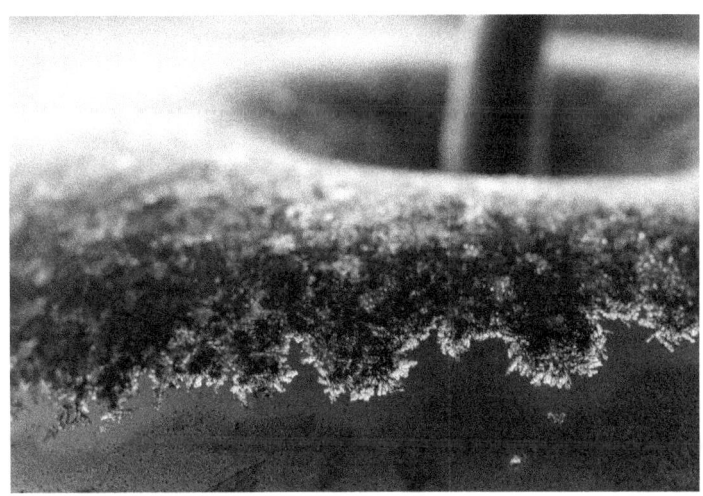

10 BELOW ZERO

An icy silhouette
against the pallid air.
The air is cold and full of snow.
Soon the apple won't be bare.

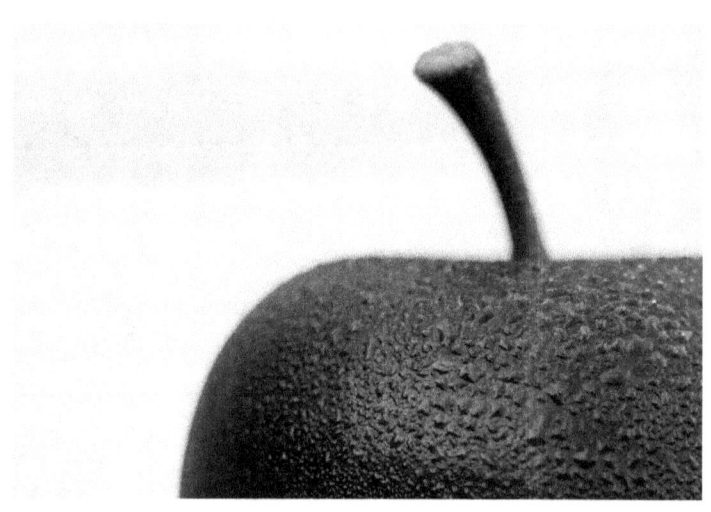

11 ICY CRYSTALS

Icy crystals along a fluid grid.
Temperature is dropping.
Every morning to my surprise
a beautiful white topping.

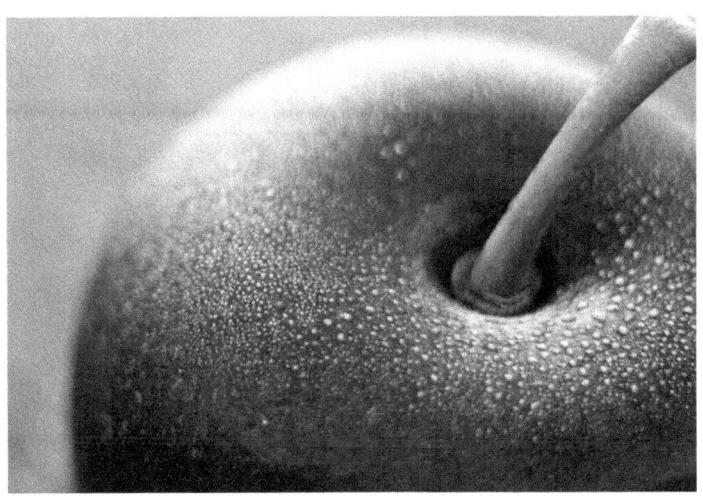

12 ICE AND SNOW

Winter is here.
Ice is covering the glass.
Longing for spring.
Oh....when will the cold weather pass?

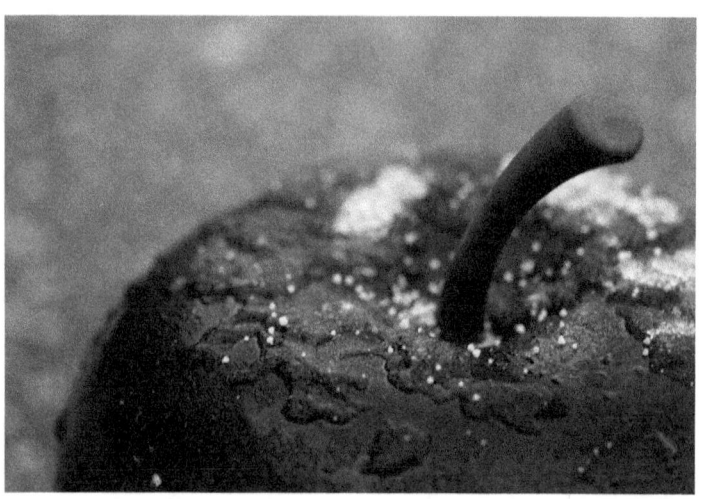

13 COVERED IN SNOW

The black is gone, the white is here
but white is not to stay.
Before you know black shines again
and white has gone away.

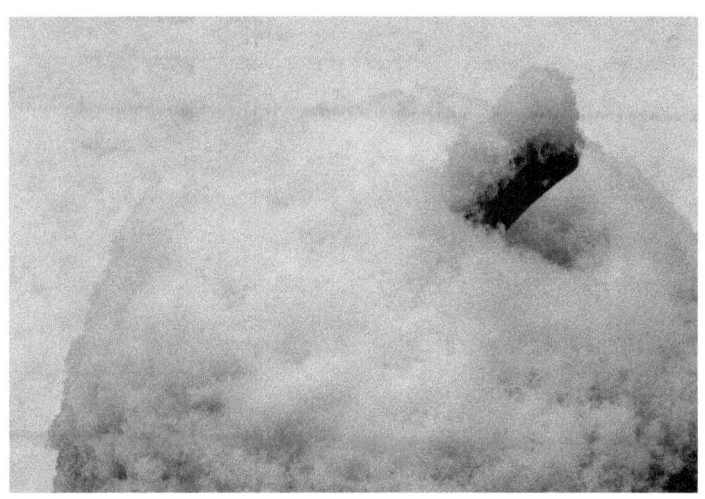

14 MELTING SNOW

Pure black and white bridged by transparent ice.
It's the metaphor of life.
Two opposites strongly connect
just like man and wife.

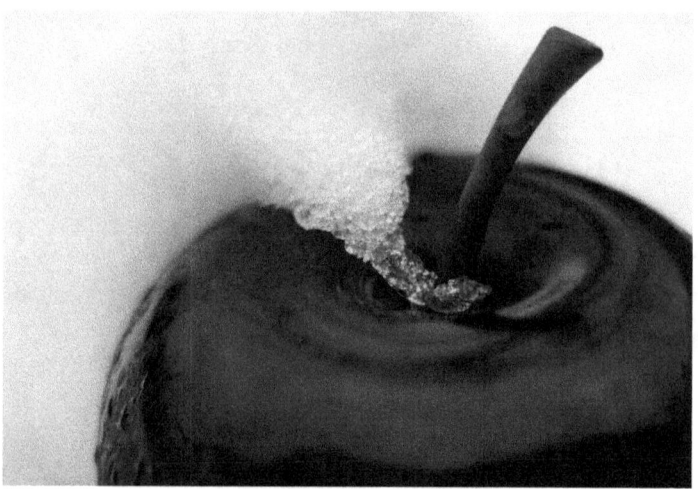

15 SLUSH

A mix of rain and snow
as if the clouds can't choose.
Will snow win this time
or is it going to lose?

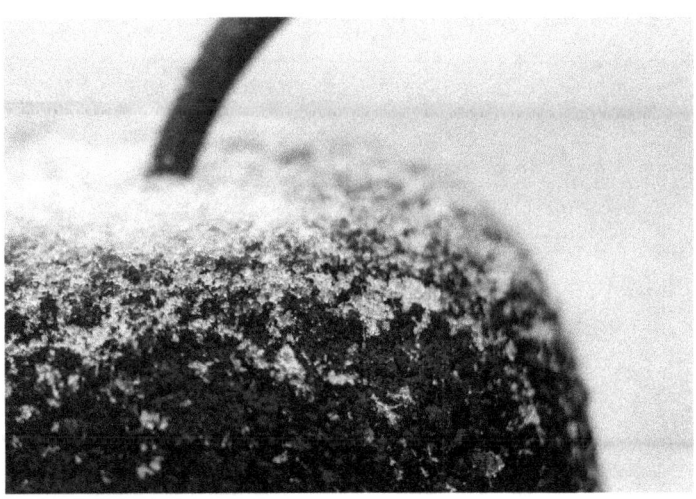

16 DUST

From a distance the apple looks shiny and clean.
Only at short range dust can be seen.
Small particles fallen down from the sky.
Only at short range they caught my eye.

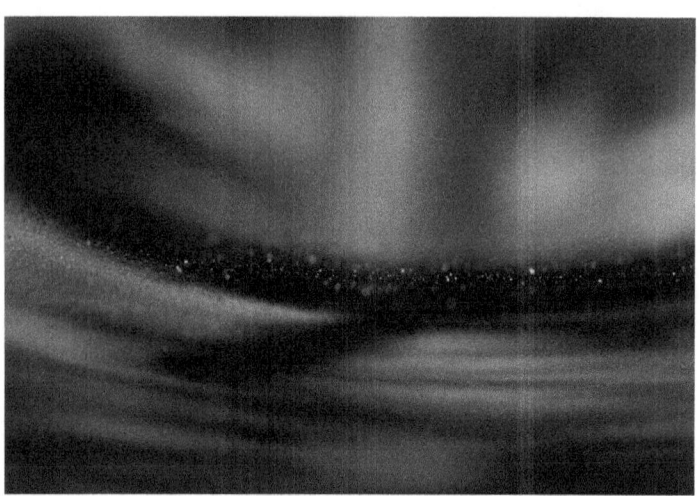

17 DIRT

After an hour of wind and rain
the black glass apple is filthy again.
What's the use of polishing
when Nature prefers a dirty thing?

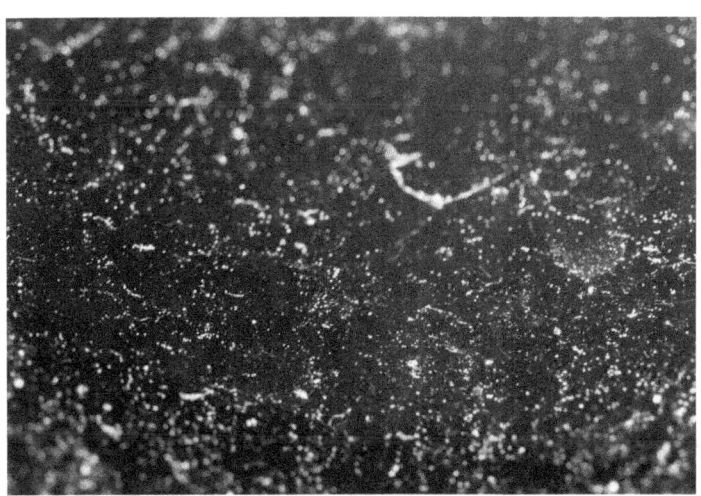

18 POLLEN

Fallen pollen
Brought by rain
Wrong location
Dropped in vain

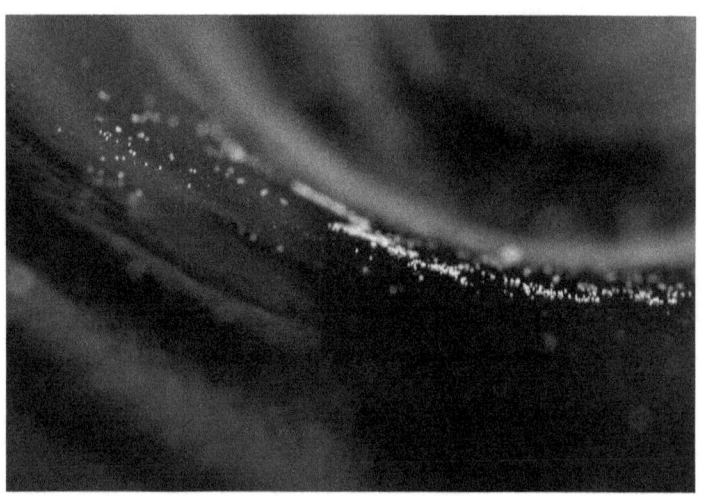

19 WALNUT

You are hiding under a walnut tree.
Bare walnut branches reflect in thee.
But spring is already in the air.
Soon branches will have leaves to bear.

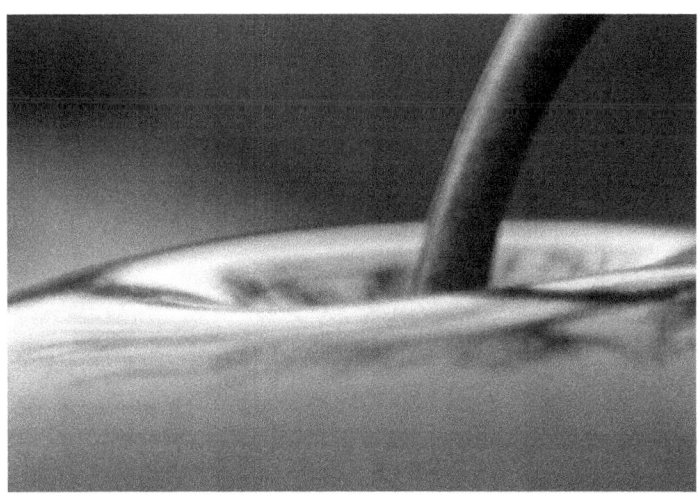

20 REFLECTION

Although an object nears perfection
that cannot be deduced from its reflection.
If a surface is rugged and rough
a reflection isn't nearly conclusive enough.

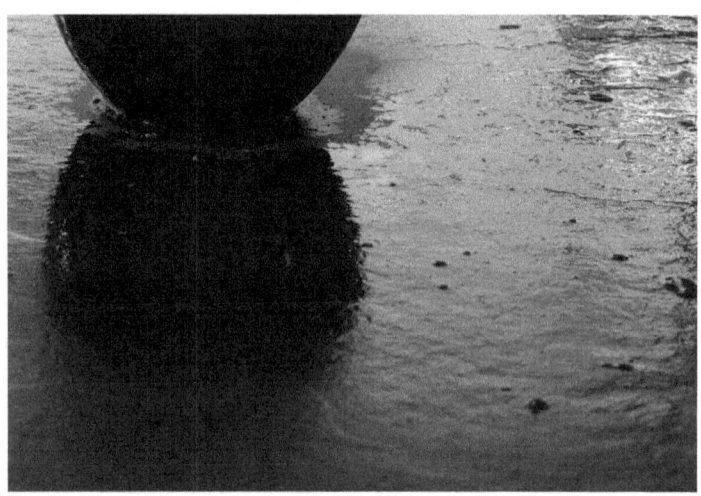

21 FROSTY REFLECTION

A walnut tree nearby
reflects in our black glass apple.
An apple bigger than a tree!
A miracle so it seems to me.

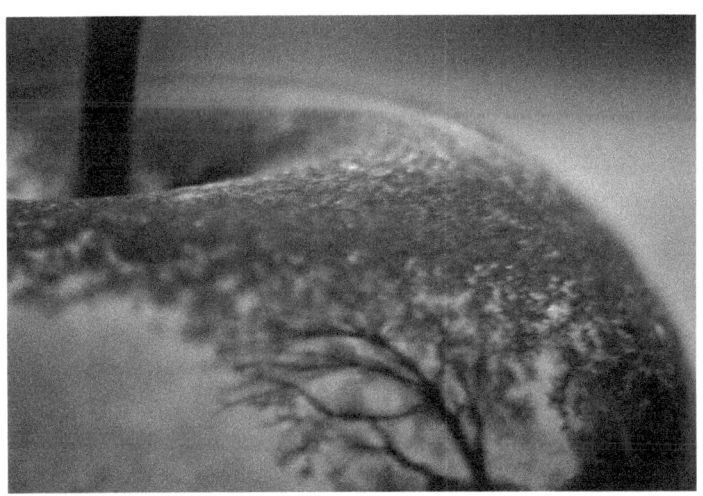

22 MORNING DEW

Precious morning dew.
When the sky is blue
and humid air is getting warm
artful drops of dew are born.

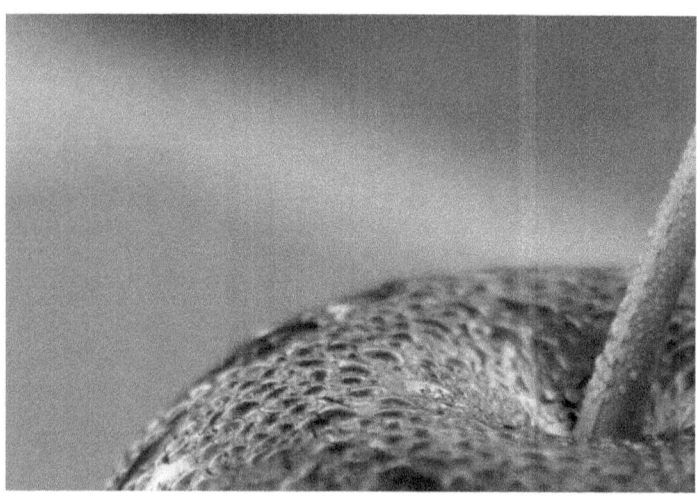

23 DAZZLING DEW

My apple is covered in diamonds.
So I am filthy rich!
A cloud, a shadow…..dark again.
The sun she is a bitch.

.

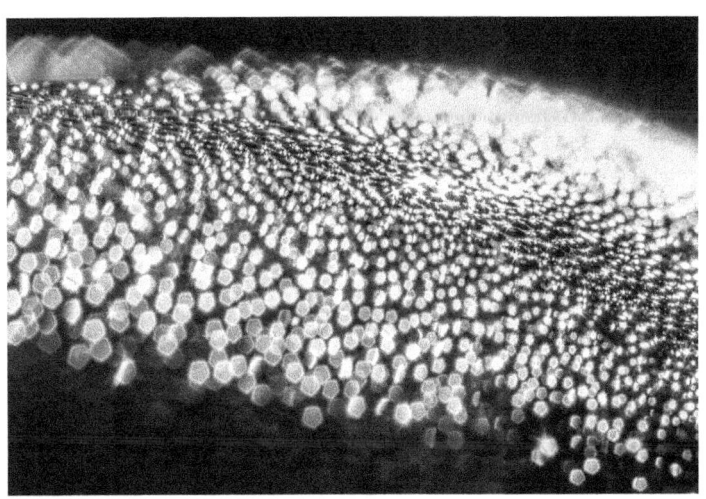

24 BLACK DEW

Black dew
Always new
Forever gone
After dawn

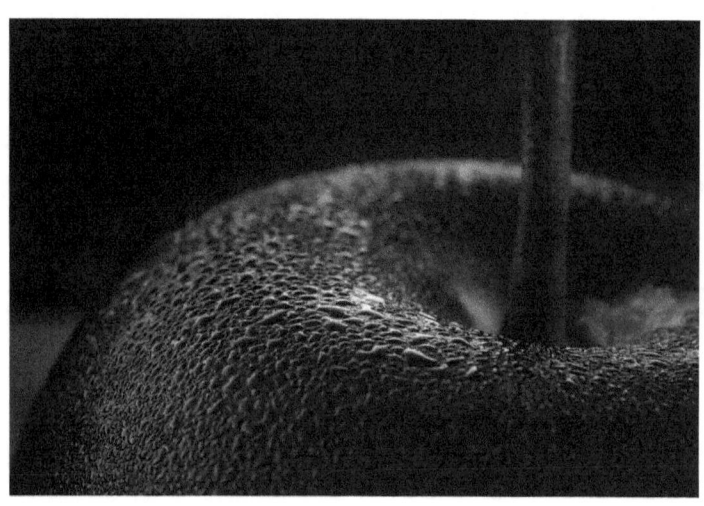

25 FROZEN DEW

Dew drops taken by surprise.
Sudden cold turned them into ice.

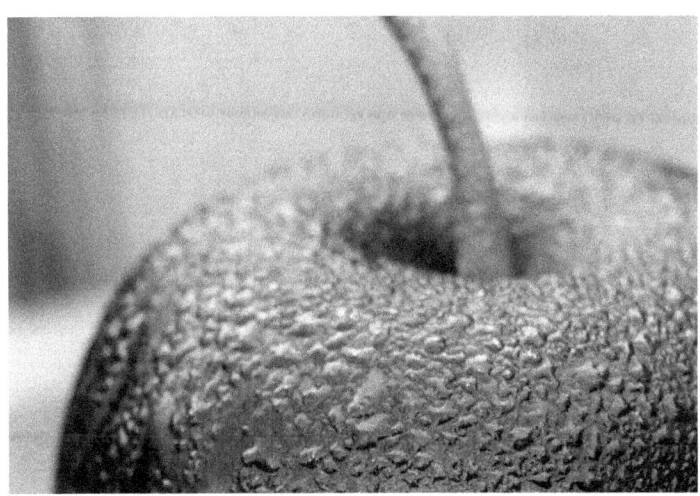

26 MOONLIGHT

Seeing dim reflections of the moon
but its light is fading soon.
Clouds approaching really fast.
Only when the storm has passed
and when time has stopped the rain
the apple reflects the light again.

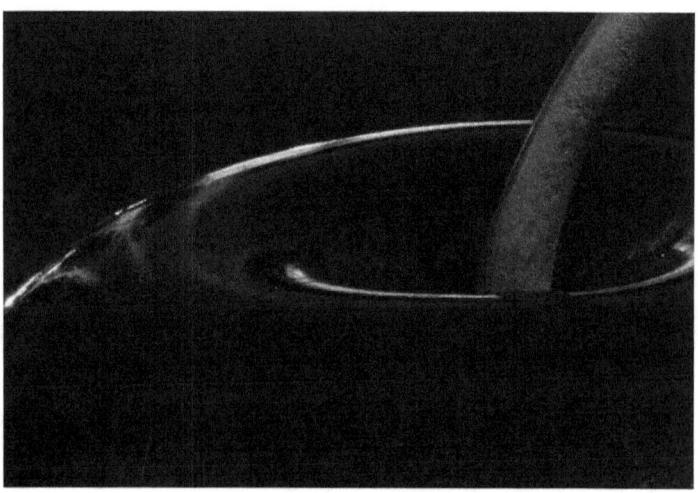

27 GARDEN LIGHTS

No poetry for garden light.
Although it lights up ev'ry night
when curtains almost are alight
and darkness fights the moon so bright

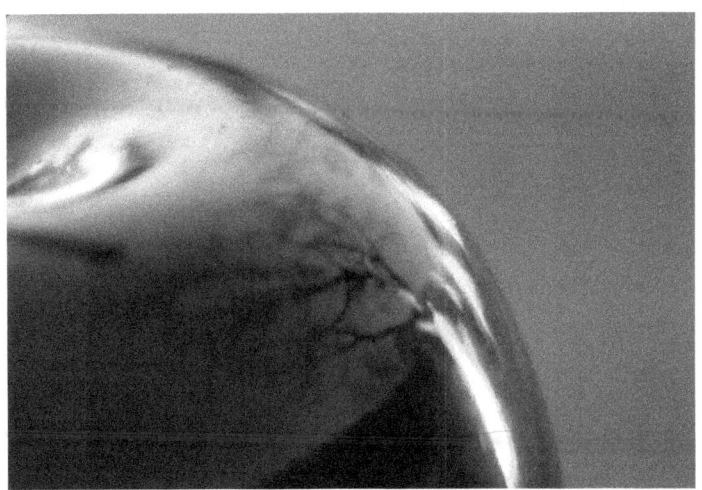

28 PITCH BLACK

No sun, no moon, no stars.
No light from Jupiter nor Mars.
No feeble flame, no glint, no spark.
A lightless night and utterly dark.
The apple shape cannot be seen
in this entirely pitch black scene.

29 SUNSET

Sunlight is slowly fading
so the reflection shows.
The light that is evading
Is one of Nature's daily shows.

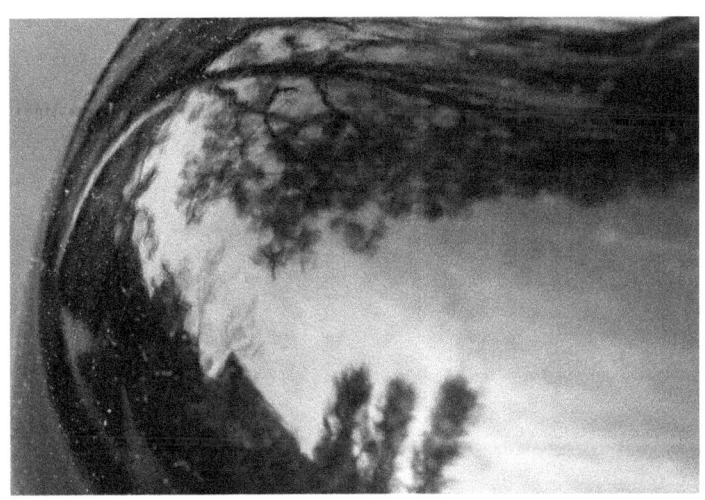

30 SHADOW

A shadow is nothing but absence of light.
Yet it needs light to exist, no shadows at night.
In Plato's cave with just shadows to see
the prisoners can't imagine what an apple would be.

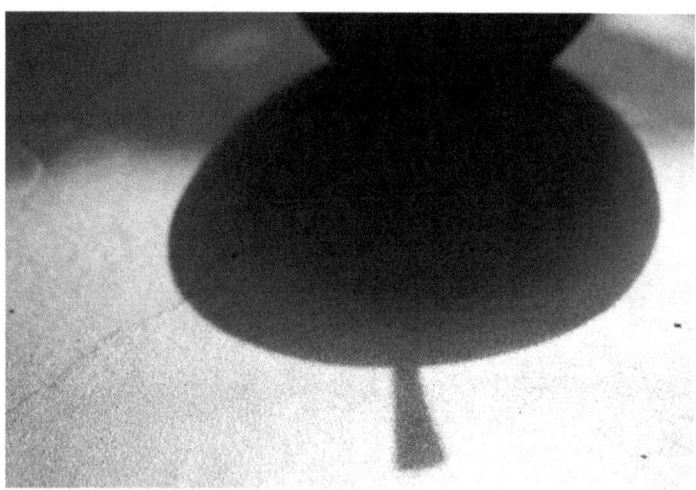

31 WASP

Last night a wasp landed on the glass.
This morning it tried to fly away.
Unless the sun will give its warmth,
evermore it's doomed to stay.

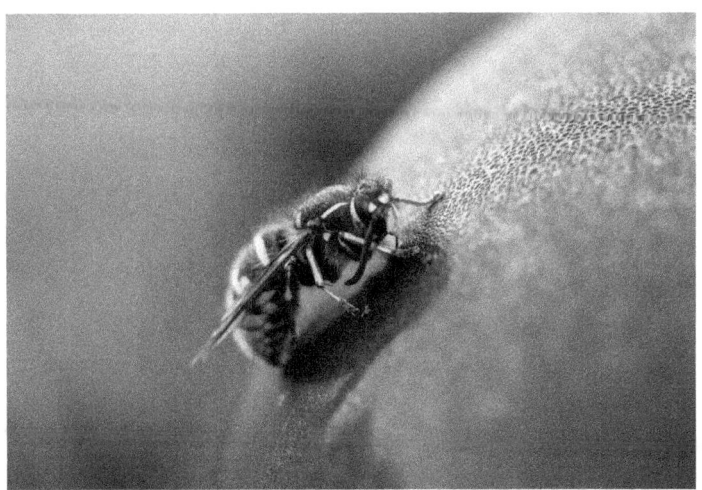

32 SPIDER

Wandering around.
Looking for a bite.
Kill without a sound.
Don't know any fright.

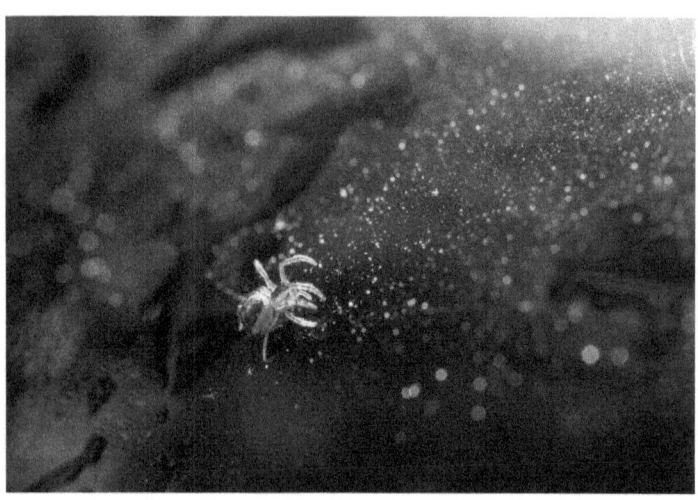

33 CATERPILLAR

A caterpillar on an apple
is quite a normal view.
What he doesn't know though
Is that on this one he cannot chew!

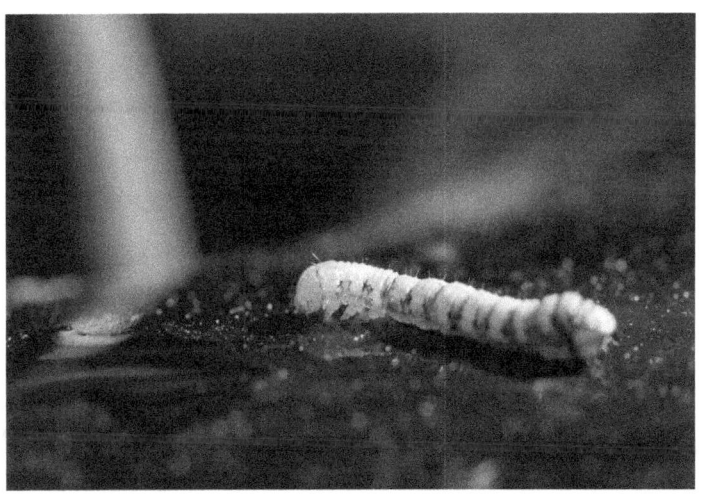

34 SNAIL

The eye of a snail is a wonder of perfection.
Can this be the result of just natural selection?
So many things need to fail to get to this brilliant
solution.
How inconceivable is Darwin's evolution!

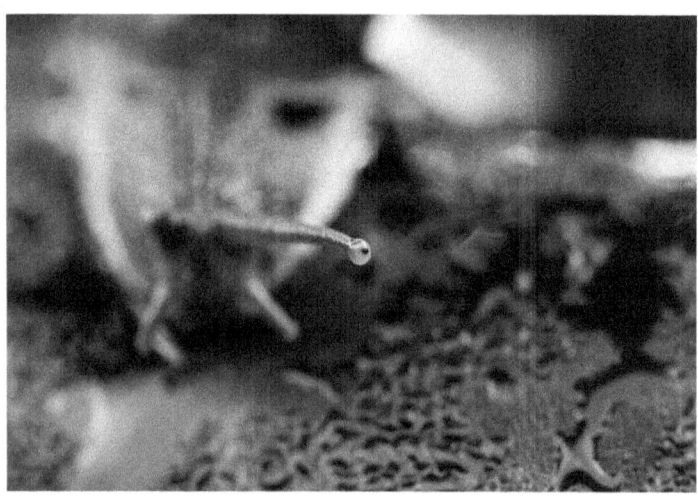

35 DEAD BODIES

A horror story on the black glass!
Two tiny corpses I have found!
Where is the culprit who has killed them?
Beware! He might be still around!

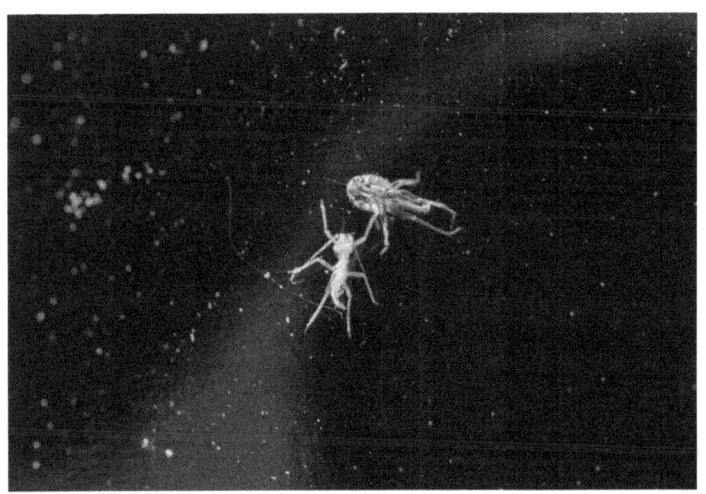

36 GERBERA DAISY

Reality or illusion?
This is so unique!
About this apple-daisy fusion
everyone will speak!

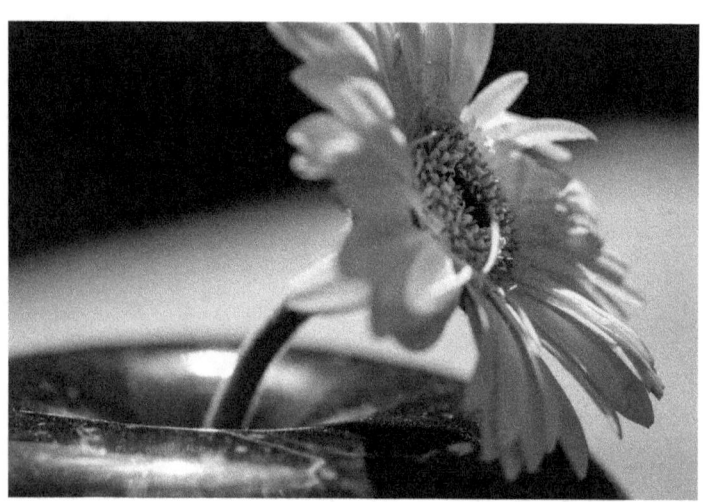

37 SILVER STRINGS

Where is the spider?
Where is the weaver?
Two filmy silver lines
are the only trailing signs.

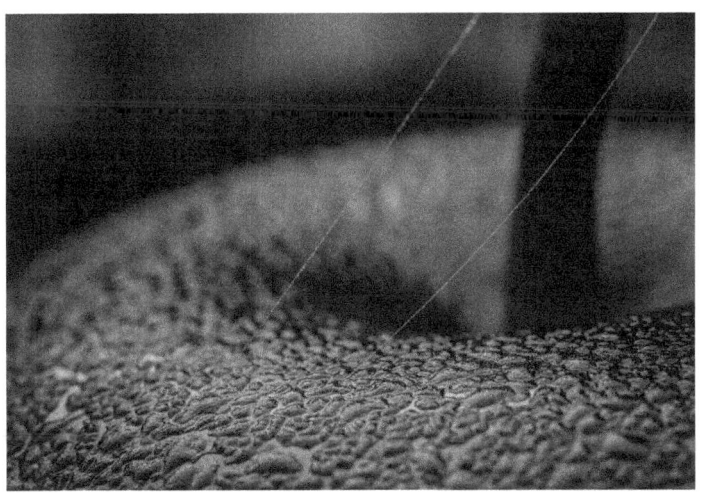

38 ACROBATS

Like acrobats on a filmy rope
Like dancers on a sticky slope.
Left-overs of a spider meal
tremble with an odd appeal.

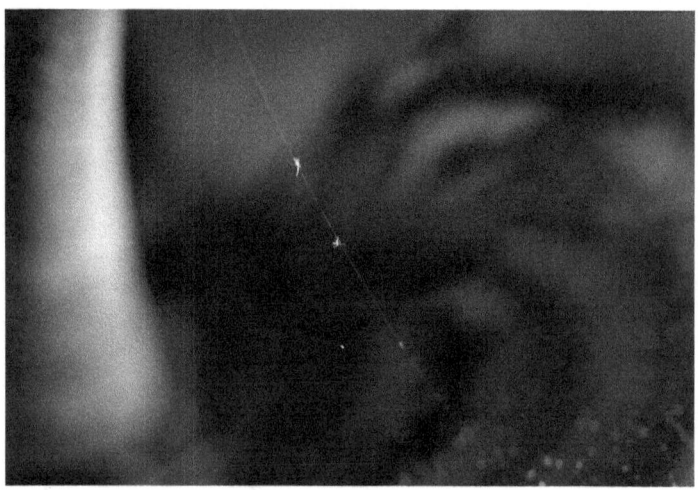

39 PIGEON SHIT

The apple took a hit
from that darned pigeon shit.
But rain will come and rinse it clean,
wash away that shitty scene.

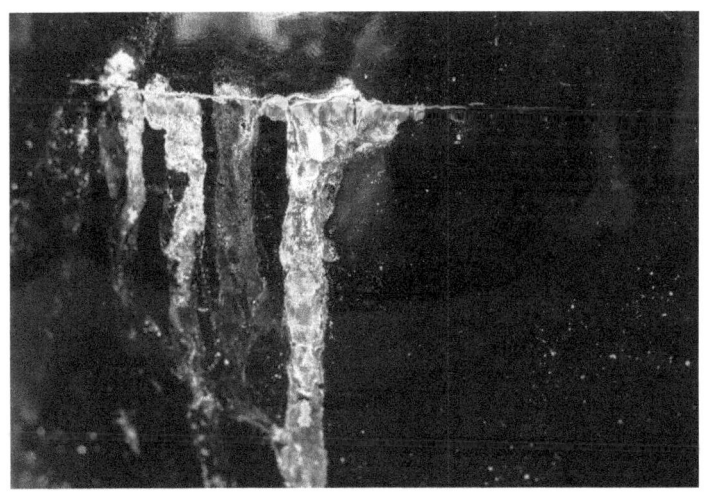

40 LEAF

"The shadow apple has grown a leaf."
A statement nobody would believe.
It clearly is just pure chance:
the leaf meeting the shadow's advance.

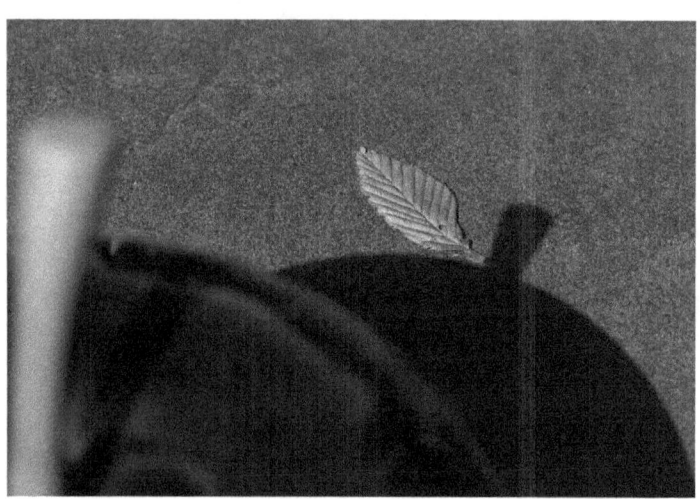

41 REAL THING

This apple here is real!
This one you can peel.
Her skin looks pinkish and her looks not shady.
I guess that's why they call her breed Pink Lady!

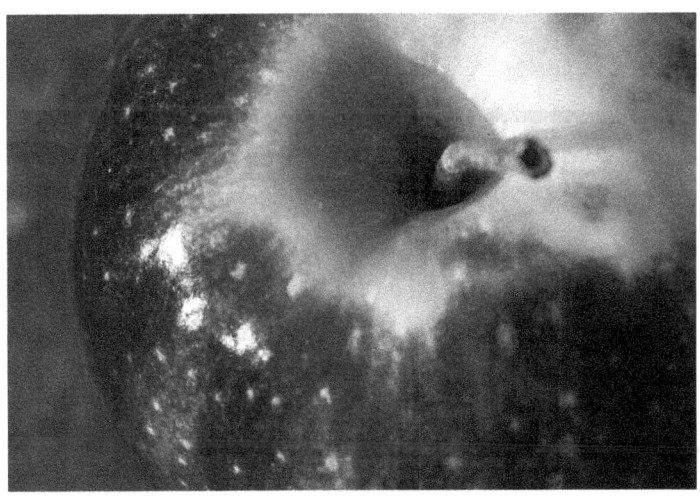

42 42

Nobody has a clue
what questions belongs to 42.
I guess Adams planned
for people to never understand.
Though some HG2G readers suspect
that the answer is in the Droste effect.
This is a most intriguing suggestion!
Suppose Droste's fixed point contains the ultimate
Question!

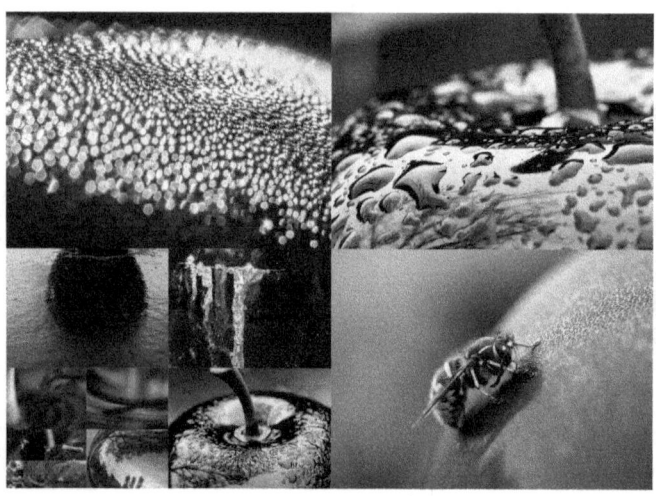

ABOUT THE AUTHOR

Well, he is just a searching soul
Without a clear perspicuous goal
With no pretension to be great
"Anonymous" will be his fate

The author fancies black and white
Albeit day, albeit night.
In close-up world where he likes to be
Amazing textures one can see

And the good old manual lens
Became one of his dearest friends
With bokeh close to buttery
His photos are a joy to see.